Throw Me An Apple

Christine Wright

Original Line Drawings by Christine Wright

First published in the UK in October 2012 by MyVoice Publishing

Copyright: © Christine Wright

Christine Wright asserts the moral right to be identified as the author of this work
Published by: MyVoice Publishing,
Unit 1,
16 Maple Road,
Eastbourne,
BN23 6NY

ISBN: 978-1-909359-01-7

All rights reserved. No part of this publication may be reproduced without the permission of the author, stored in a retrieval system, or transmitted, in any form or by any means, electronic, mechanical, photocopying, recording or otherwise, without the permission of the publisher.

This book is sold subject to the condition that it shall not, by way of trade or otherwise, be lent, re-sold, hired out or otherwise circulated without the publisher's prior consent in any form of binding or cover other than that in which it is published and without a similar condition including this condition being imposed on the subsequent purchaser.

Christine Wright

Contents

Prams   3

Food   15

Animals   26

Visitors   45

Cars   59

You gave me some of my sunniest days   67

Fire and water   77

Surprises, gifts and games   88

Throw Me An Apple

Christine Wright

Prams

The problem is, you see, if you don't write things down, you forget them. Some things, of course, are just as well dispensed with in this way, but there are a few things that would be sadly missed, and my life at least would have very definitely been a rather grey affair without them.

It's really just a question of where to begin, and at this stage, I really hope that the trickle of colour and excitement, happiness and occasional quiet moments trapped in my memory, will become a raging torrent, pouring through the pages of my book.

Being a mother (Mum for short) of quite a collection of children, prams have played rather an indelibly important role in my life. Prams have been used for some ingenious, not to say amazing services, but mainly of course, transporting the latest addition around. Not every latest addition has actually managed to remain "inside" the pram, strange to say.

In my earlier years when my own physical weight was considerably less, a horrifying event took place. Not so horrifying to me, I must add, not the occupants of the huge coach-built pram, but for the dear elderly lady accompanying me on that wet and miserable day, a spectacle I doubt she ever really recovered from.

As I said, the rain was torrential and consequently three year old twins and a six month babe were tucked cosily under the hood of this giant contraption. What a brainwave, home and dry in no time. First though, we had to descend three steep steps leaving a block of flats. To bounce the pram down on the wheels nearest the handle could have buckled them and the twins could have shot through the hood with the impact, so the obvious answer was to lower the pram front wheels first!!!

I am sure, even to this day, no girl as inexperienced as I was at the time, could possibly have foreseen the consequences of the following few seconds. Front wheels firmly down, the handle slowly began to ascend, gaining rapid momentum heavenward. I discreetly shuffled my legs to try to add extra weight to balance the pram and contents. Within seconds, all control lost, I was kicking wildly in the most undignified way, yelling for help, whilst I continued to ascend helpless, my children looking on, mesmerised from under the hood, at the pillar of stability in their lives having totally lost control of the situation, legs waving wildly for some minutes, before the pram finally came to rest up end, on its hood, and the only way for me to return to terra firma by the shortest route was to let go of the handle at once. This done, I landed in a crumpled heap, embarrassed to say the least, dignity non-existent, sheepish and stricken with shock. But my condition was one of ecstasy compared with my companion, her poor face was the absolute picture of horror and astonishment; it was clear that never before had she experienced such an event. Don't actually recall being in her company again.

My prams were always, with the occasional exception, of the gigantic variety due to the abundance of children in transit. There was always a baby, often a couple of toddlers and small children scattered around the handles and whatever else they could hang on to as we went on our way.

"Our Way" was frequently expeditions into the countryside, the beach, their Auntie's five miles away or wherever I felt their lives would be enhanced by experiencing the wonders of the world we live in.

The pram on these occasions would be loaded in the very early morning with apples, wholemeal bread, cheese,

Christine Wright

Throw Me An Apple

oatcakes or maybe a giant fruitcake, a gallon of water in a container always dwelt on the luggage rack ready for these excursions, football, swim suits, bats of every description and of course, nappies.

Long summer days were spent in these wanderings and the baby of the moment perched on top of all this like the king of the castle, brown as a berry and bursting with health. These were the "contents" of our picnic days out, and this unsophisticated lifestyle was all the children knew for years.

Eventually one of the oldest was invited picnicking with friends and came home with tales of enlightenment, having had the picnic of a lifetime, actually on a table-cloth, with, wait for it!!! wine, chicken, a variety of cheeses etc., etc., and of all things, PLATES and a CUP EACH!!!

Returning on the homeward stretch after adventuring was usually a quiet, peaceful and drowsy affair - we always took the country route, and strolled contentedly toward dusk. The picnic long gone, the pram was generally loaded now with the youngest and the tiredest members, baby sound asleep, taking turns on the luggage tray underneath. An idyllic picture, all peace, sun burnt and rosy faces, grubby happy tee shirts, wilting bouquets of wild flowers and sweet sleep beckoning all, when suddenly and without warning, the loudest screeching and howling of "stop, stop, help, help," "get me out, it's got my hair". Number four, a beautiful child with an abundance of black flowing hair and a deeply ingrained, lazy streak, coupled with a domineering "I want to ride on the luggage rack" attitude, had finally got her wish. Having turned to cast her conquerors grin at the walkers, and gloat over her rather elevated, albeit close to the ground situation, her flowing locks had rapidly entangled themselves into the hub of the right front wheel and she was hysterically envisioning the shredding of her head perhaps, followed by the rest of her through the spokes.

I was more horrified by the various contents already established on that well-worn wheel, this was not the sort of pram solely used on clean pavements. Horses, cows, etc. had often used the lanes before us and I clearly had some washing of hair to do when we arrived home, but the job at hand was disentangling this howling and distraught individual. Of course, all ended well, we got her out in the end. She very politely offered her place on the luggage rack to one of her siblings. What a charitable gesture from one so young!!!
Her flowing locks suffered no ill effects. They are still quite spectacular.

As I have previously hinted, not all my infants managed to actually remain "inside" the pram. The bigger the pram it seems, the more spectacular the unexpected exit. One star-spangled event took place outside a country pub at mid-afternoon closing time. Several people were making their way out and home in various stages of intoxication, when my husband and I plus two sleeping babes and proverbial prams shot the pub hastily heading for home, some distance still, in time for our brood coming home from school. Youngest babe slept soundly at the handle end of the pram whilst his still tiny sister slept soundly at the opposite end. We flew past the pub entrance, down the pavement edge onto the driveway, up the opposite pavement but alas disaster struck. Two wheels on the left landed securely on the pavement, two wheels on the right, sad to say, did nothing of the kind. Memories poured into my desperate mind as the pram uncontrollably listed to the right.

Distraught Father, too far away to help, a pram too intent on discharging its contents and a, by now, large group of intoxicated country people gazing in drunken disbelief as the only assistance I can give my baby boy is my leg to roll down, and his sister opposite, my sincere desire that her landing won't be too bumpy on this occasion.

Things weren't too tragic, I'm relieved to relate. Naturally they both woke up and howled in shock and we bumped into each other in our haste to gather up our somewhat distraught offspring and deal with that disgusting rebellious pram, which was still refusing to stand on four wheels like its contemporaries, but then it had had a rather hard and strenuous life.

The two in the pram on that occasion were my last daughter number seven and her baby brother number eight. Both were close in age and have remained close in affection, and both spent quite a lot of time in that aforementioned mode of transport, him cosily under the hood in winter, and her swathed and bound in blankets, woollies and a sleeping bag wedged onto the pram seat. They spent a lot of time that way, talking in their own words to each other, holding hands, although on one snowy evening, there was a temporary gap in their togetherness.

Snow was laying thick, an unusual occurrence in our region. We were leaving a friend's house and it was dark. Number eight was seated in his usual pride of place in the pram on top of the resident hot water bottle. Number seven was wrapped in even more blankets than usual, topped over all with a white sleeping bag, a truly unfortunate choice of colour on this particular occasion, because no sooner has she been placed on her seat, even before her position could be secured, in fact within seconds, she had quite disappeared into the snow covered garden without trace. Her brother looked perplexed and was peering over the edge of his pram in disbelief. It had all happened so fast. A kind of silent body roll into white obscurity. All we could do was feel for the bit of "white" that wasn't cold, and we eventually picked her out of the rose bush, unharmed once

Christine Wright

more and strangely oblivious, sort of resigned to her fate in her quiet way.

Numerous items have been transported by "pram" over the years. In the very early years, the last knockings of a household removal brought a particularly gallant and stalwart double hooded affair to an inglorious conclusion, spokes pinging and listing badly, it was wheeled rather unceremoniously to the local tip and a last glance at my old comrade brought back the memories of those former days. The twins that used to occupy its great cosy interior. And if that pram could speak, it would no doubt howl with laughter.

From the moment this pair were aware of each other's existence, some dissension took place. Vigorous kicking, that I felt would cease when they sat up, dedicated hair pulling commenced, plus pinching and poking of every description to the point of my having to devise a barrier between the two.

Their teddy bear rattles, however, overcame all barriers and the battle commenced, pink and blue teddies waved relentlessly and had to be confiscated for their own protection. When one twin smiled, the other howled and when one spat a mouthful of food, the other found a handful of the stuff could do just as much, if not more, damage.

The twins' next mode of transport was the twin-pushchair which of course didn't have the stability of "old-faithful?" and when the shopping bags were heaped onto the handles, the contraption had to be held onto every second. Occasionally, of course, one would forget, but the momentary relapse would soon be heralded by a howling and hysterical pair, and the sight of four small legs kicking wildly in the air, items of groceries and fruit rolling about the pavement and bemused passers-by watching in disbelief.

For occasions like this, I usually had a secret ally. "The penny lollipop" could cure ills, sometimes I ate one myself. What I really needed was brandy but one has to make do with what is available at the time.

We had just semi-survived a fiasco similar to the one related above, we were actually waiting in a bus queue when this all took place. I recall the eggs that were deliberately rolled into the gutter by my two angels behind my back, whilst I was mentally sympathising with the "poor soul" who had lost her eggs in the gutter, having no idea she was me. We boarded the bus, one had a yellow lolly, one had a green one and I hoped for an uneventful journey home. With a bundle of joy on each knee and both arms totally occupied, I smiled at the person opposite who smiled back because she was watching the angels twisting their lollies into my long black hippie hair and there wasn't a single thing I could do about it. The silver lining was I didn't live far from the bus stop.

I did something special for the twins when they were tiny, their bedroom. I moved them out and painted giant murals of lovable bunnies and mice, flowers of all descriptions, grass and trees. I was delighted.

Their cots were prepared, all their toys set out and the moment of the unveiling of the projects of a lifetime was imminent. The twins were given tea, bathed, cuddled, nappied and carried up the stairs to their nursery haven. Popped into their cots, they stood clinging to the sides and gazing in astonishment. "Well~" I thought "it's certainly had an impact on their little minds". Suddenly, all hell broke loose, and they screamed and howled in abject horror and had to be rushed downstairs for a lolly. The whole incident had a somewhat dampening effect on my artistic fervour, but glad to say that they did get used to it, and seemed to like it in the end.

Throw Me An Apple

Christine Wright

My prams and pushchairs have suffered a variety of fates over the years. One or two, I'm rather ashamed to say, collapsed in total immobility and had to be abandoned to serve out their end as discreetly as possible supporting a hedge. My guilt over the dumping of these articles plagued me, but have you ever tried hauling a crippled and collapsed pushchair whose wheels refuse to revolve, whilst supporting a bouncing babe under one arm, who suddenly appears to weigh several tons, at least one carrier bag, coats and spare woollies, plus try to gather the assortment of smaller children who now find a new freedom and scatter because "the handle", the nucleus of orderly walking procedure is now sitting in a hedge waiting to be the support of baby robins perhaps. Probably a welcome change from the previous occupant.
Occasionally pushchairs in particular have momentarily rebelled and actually folded the occupant up in a neat envelope arrangement, which is quite dreadful, of course, but really the sight of the disappearing handle followed by the view of those little arms and legs protruding, the top of a curly head and the muffled yells coming from somewhere within would have me in tears of laughter every time.

I think though, the most anxiety is experienced when the slow disintegration of those large coach-built stalwarts begins whilst in transit. That awful pinging of spokes that no easing down pavements seems to prevent. That look of creeping insecurity on the face of the occupant as the place of security begins to list and lean badly, and the hedgerows and streams look so much closer now. And by the way, why has Muv got that sickly smile, trying to hide that look of resignation.

Our very last family pram gasped its last in this way, and I insisted on a photograph when the nearside wheel finally subsided and insisted on taking up a horizontal position which no amount of bits of string and kicking or begging would correct.

It was all over, and loaded with picnic leftovers, cricket equipment, football, coats, woollies, etc. we limped home on three wheels, and number eight had to use his legs long distance for the first time. The end of an era.

Christine Wright

Food

Food, of course, has played something of a starring role in the course of our history. The acquiring of, the cooking of, occasionally a slight scarcity of, the appreciation of, when available, and the content of some saucepans produced in our kitchen would, I am sure, raise the eyebrows of the gourmet. On reflection, the family has, over the years, silently endured some rather obscure food combinations, the odd culinary disaster and an abundance of baked potatoes. I have concluded: they must be endowed with a cast iron constitution, determination of solid steed and a deep love for me and respect for my feelings.

Food, when free for the picking variety was available, we rather made the most of it. Blackberries, consequently, turned up in pies, jellies, yoghurt and trifle. They lurked at the bottom of cakes sometimes, to bemuse the guest and embarrass the more sophisticated members of the family.

They were crammed by the handful into gaping mouth of one particular blackberry enthusiast, who sat in her pram whilst the rest of the family gathered the abundant crop, howling when her mouth was empty and having it crammed full by whoever was closest to the din she made.

I often wonder how many little maggots she consumed with all that fruit, when I went on the principle of one every four or five berries. I had to cease to contemplate and let her get on with it. I was always quite astonished that she suffered no ill effects, just sat there, turning gradually more purple as the juice ran, and squiddging a few into her hair and pram as she became bored with waiting for us all.

Other obscure objects, some alive, were consumed by this

particular, rather eccentric little person. I discovered her "taste of the unusual" when half a wood louse turned up in the bib of her dungarees. I had heard that some tiny tots do this, but it was a first for me, and she was number five. Always curious, and interested this one, always the first to try it out, a fast moving unsinkable live wire, who innocently persecuted her baby brother. This one a quiet intense little soul frequently submerged and swallowed up in her whirlwind activity.

A large and hairy caterpillar actually suffered the same fate quite literally at her hands. One moment she was stroking it, the next she was screaming for me to "get its hair out" of her mouth, but it was too late, the caterpillar's fate was sealed and for weeks later she screamed every time she saw one.

Enquiries were once made by one of the middle children as to what the black and whites bits on the floor under the budgie's cage actually were. I explained in child's terms they were the birdie's droppings and she explained in no uncertain terms that number five eats them. This time I was rigid with horror. Once more I marvelled after recovering from the shock, at this bundle of health, energy and vigour and wondered how on earth she maintained that blooming rosy appearance on her chosen diet.

As I have said, when food for some reason came free, we made the absolute most of it, evident by jars and jars of mainly blackberry, damson, apple or a mixture of apple and cinnamon, apple and ginger, to try to disguise the persistent re-appearance of apple. There was a rhubarb era too and it would have lasted longer if a rebellion of rather serious proportions hadn't broken out, rhubarb was off. Apples though seem to have stood the test of time and we still feel more secure if the great bread basket under the kitchen table is full of them.

Christine Wright

Throw Me An Apple

We have always had to, of necessity, buy in bulk, whenever possible. We were accustomed to that and quite forgot most people's purchases are made by the pound or so - this is normal.

On one of our wanderings through the country lanes of our beautiful locality, and during a particularly financially Spartan time of our history, we passed a cottage, in the garden of which, grew an apple tree. The apples were in abundance, in the tree, on the ground below, more than a beautiful, beautiful sight and all the way home I just couldn't bear the thought of all that obviously delicious waste while our apple basket lay empty.

I made a decision and some of the older children went to make some discreet enquiries on my behalf. The owners, who were only too happy to have them go to good use, told the children to bring something to put them in and help themselves. I was more than thrilled - the thought of sending them with a couple of carrier bags or boxes didn't even enter my head. "TAKE THE PRAM MY DEARS". The huge coach-built disappeared into the country lane and returned loaded with its delicious, not to say, priceless cargo and a message: "you may as well come and get the rest!!!" No sooner said than done, and another excursion was made. Was even more wonderful and a bonus for a certainty was the fact that they were absolutely delicious.

Some days later there was a knock at my door. I opened it to a woman with two giant marrows in her hands. "Are you the lady with eight children?" she said, hardly able to contain her laughter. "Yes" I replied. "Well, I'm the apple lady" she said, bursting into laughter and gave me the marrows. We both laughed and I thanked her as she departed.

Some days later still, a man stopped me not too far from my front gate. "Excuse me dear. Are you the lady with eight children?" I looked at the large box of mixed vegetables in his arms, then at him, and we both burst out laughing. "Well, I'm the apple man" he said. I have never seen them since, but they were some of the "colour" in a grey time.

Our apple and blackberry pies in season were of truly immense proportions by average standards. The children and maybe a couple of their friends would be out harvesting the blackberries whilst I whacked together the pastry. The apples were chopped - there never seemed time to peel them - and all the children, plus friends, crammed into my tiny kitchen to watch the proceeds of their labour transformed. Then later when it was time for the whole, sugared, steaming, delicious smelling end product to emerge from the oven, back they all came to sample all our efforts and carry some off as spoil for their Mums to try.

Some of my cakes were a different story!!! There was always a fruit cake, in fact still is, and it has often been part of our staple diet, together with the baked potatoes and apples. The method of producing these cakes amazed a few of our newer or more fleeting acquaintances, old friends were more stalwart and unshakable, having become immune over the years to some of our, more of necessity, eccentric ways.

I had long abandoned the standard mixing bowl for a small baby's bath, which sometimes had to double as other things. Potatoes were often soaked and scrubbed in it and so were the odd pair of socks, but survive we have and with a vengeance. The cakes were baked finally in roasting tins or either of my old steamers, and still are.

An extraordinary thing happened to one of my banana cakes. I'm sure an expert would put their finger on the problem in no time. We were merely bemused when it re-appeared from the oven about one third of the size it had

Throw Me An Apple

entered there. What was to be done with it? Nothing of an edible nature was ever, ever wasted, but really, did this object come into the category edible.

There was a family debate and it was decided (not unanimously I must add) that we should at least try. It was of the consistency of a tractor tyre. Having taken a slice and bitten into it, it simply refused to dissolve in your mouth. Swallowing it would have been an act of gross irresponsibility. It sat on the kitchen table for a couple of days unchanged, until the final decision was made to give it to the chickens. Everything went to the chickens and they dutifully ploughed through all leftovers. Given the opportunity they ploughed through mine and my neighbour's garden flowers too, but that's another.

A procession of children bore the "cake" to its final resting place, or so we thought and they stood and watched as the chickens slowly came to investigate. The chickens seemed a bit slow on the uptake, it was clearly going to be a little while before they decided it was to be eaten and the children gradually lost interest and came indoors.

The weather was bad for the next couple of weeks, lots of rain, and restlessness and boredom slowly descended. Finally things brightened up and we all recovered from the doldrums. "Pop out and see if the chickens finished off that cake, there's a dear". One of the children disappeared. She returned with a look of amusement and a touch of disbelief on her face. "It's still there" she said, "and one of 'ems sitting on it". We all rolled up at that and tried to work out whether they thought it was a cushion or was she perhaps trying to hatch it out!!!

Free food was especially appreciated in the lean times and on odd occasions some recycling went on. Number five by the age of three was an avid follower of the pick it and eat

Throw Me An Apple

it association. All varieties of food were joy to her and in order to maintain peace, we were in the habit of feeding the brute. Figs, berries, crusts of bread and fruit, handfuls of raisins disappeared rapidly and more was demanded.

Number five discovered paradise on one of our walks. We had stopped for a while by some grazing sheep, peaceful, totally harmless surroundings, nothing can happen here, relax, re-charge your batteries and what is that child clutching in her hand. "What is it dear?" "Raisins everywhere Mummy." "STOP! They are not raisins, put that down at once". That's another year off my life. "Can somebody explain to that child they're sheep's droppings? I've had enough for one day."

Over the years, we've tried various "hedgerow nourishment" - not all of it successful. The nettles were, well, I suppose, a total disaster, and the acorns were a non-starter, even roasted. There just seemed such a lot lying around at the time and on the principle, "it's worth a try" we tried and I must add we failed.

On one occasion some leftover flour and water wallpaper paste had to be recycled into pancakes and one horrified guest to tea has never forgotten that occasion.

Fried potato scones that have smoked out the house, destroyed the frying pan and tried my long suffering family to the limits, gravy that has turned to tadpoles before my very eyes and hard-boiled eggs that exploded and burned, and lots more. No wonder we all settle for potatoes in their jackets so readily. Better the devil you know.

By some strange irony, we seem to have been acquainted with an abundance of chefs and super cooks and have spent much of my time during their visits deviously sneaking in and out of the kitchen to prepare their meals in strict privacy.

Throw Me An Apple

There have been numerous offers of assistance that I have politely turned down and fled to my domain. What none of them realised was that if I never saw a kitchen again, I would be the happiest woman in the world.

One chef visitor actually sneaked into the kitchen after me when a curry was being prepared. Well, I think he sneaked anyway. "I've never seen a curry prepared in that way before", he said, as every ingredient was hastily flung into a giant saucepan simultaneously. "This is the quick way dear" was my reply. "Sit down, I'll make you a nice drink." I think he needed it to get over the shock.

"What on earth are you doing with that poor chicken?" enquired another well intentioned friend who had crept stealthily up behind me and caught me in the process of unceremoniously throwing the naked bird onto the bare bars of the cooker, unbasted and unprotected in any way, to fend for itself. "Oh, it'll be O.K." I assured her. We ate the rather stringy results later, whilst my family were cast sympathetic glances from my super-cook friend. I'm really happy to say, she still thinks the world of me, and I think she's accepted, after all these years, that my efforts in the kitchen will probably remain of a very basic nature. Probably why we're all so fond of apples!!

Animals

Let sleeping dogs lie! But do you think the husband would listen? Oh no. Sheba was an Alsatian of average to large proportions, who always slept across the threshold of the kitchen door because nobody argued with her often. The husband was resolved to eat his dinner on his lap in front of the TV this time, so a journey from kitchen to lounge with loaded plate was called for. Fair enough, millions of people do this.

I suggested stepping over the sleeping dog and he agreed. However, the best laid plans can go awry. As he was stepping over the dog, in fact in mid-step, he suddenly ordered her to get up, and by some unexpected twist of fate, she actually obeyed on this occasion. It was unbelievable, husband, plate, knife and fork, bangers, mash, etc. - all flew into the air simultaneously, parted company and went their separate ways. The plate smashed, the knife and fork were last seen trying to get out the back door, the bangers took refuge under a put-u-up and the husband, ah, the husband … he went right into orbit, hovered for a second or two and made a curious crash landing.

His knee broke his fall, but sad to say it landed on his finger. Thirteen stone of body falling from a dizzy height onto his finger end and he was back on his feet in no time, howling and leaping through the house in excruciating pain, his finger getting blacker by the minute.

What comfort could one bring to this poor man? The finger was probably broken, the knee wasn't far off it, the big race on TV was virtually over and man's best friend had retrieved, and was making short work of man's lunch, not that the escapee sausages could have been salvaged anyway, they had acquired a fair old fur coat on their journey through

"Everything flew up into the air and parted company"

space and time. Old Sheba wasn't moulting for nothing.

The husband has a passion for reptiles that has been passed onto his sons. All creatures that creep, crawl, slither, spit and drool are regarded by them as objects of wonder and beauty.

Over the years, I have managed to suppress my horror and repulsion at such things and accept my lot in life with as much dignity as possible. I have watched my infant rush out of the back door into the garden, day in and day out, at the crack of dawn. His objective? To push over the garden bench, scoop up the inhabitants of that dark, damp and gruesome little kingdom existing beneath, and bring as many specimens as he could to meet his Mother. If I was vigilant and fast enough, I could thwart his endeavours at the back door, and have him unhand the beasts.

I have gazed from my kitchen window at number five, when a tiny girl, and watched her gently caressing and cooing to one of God's creatures held close to her chest! On closer inspection, I have discovered the recipient of her affections has been a large, gluey, slimy, orange and brown slug attached firmly to her jumper. I just counted my blessings it was still stuck to her jumper, this little lovely was in the habit of eating such things.

Frogs, toads and slow worms, we have received hospitably on numerous occasions and some have tried to take up permanent residence. Particularly was this the case with five slow worms in a box. They didn't like it in the box. One almost made its getaway through a tiny hole in a quilted bedspread. The bedspread still being used as a bedspread at the time. The remainder were put into a box to return to a field directly. The box and contents were shortly taken and the children returned to tell me they had tipped a box of grass out into the field. No sign of a slow worm.

Christine Wright

"HE WAS COILED UP UNDER THE TOWEL"

It got progressively worse as lizards and grass-snakes were introduced into the family circle. None of these creatures enjoyed captivity and escaped frequently, spending more time slithering around the house than being restrained in their allocated dwelling area.

Their food was equally rebellious and we soon had crickets chirping in most bedrooms and particularly behind the freezer. If nothing else, they gave the house a kind of tropical atmosphere.

The grass snakes were particularly sneaky and found they could easily blend in with the logs in the log pile in the lounge, and remain there fairly indefinitely. I found in the end, it was as well not to even try to explain to our visitors. The stories and explanations became so complicated and even having convinced them that they were not in any way poisonous, I still couldn't guarantee that one would not suffer a heart attack if our pets appeared unexpected from under the sofa or somewhere. I settled for hoping for the best, and being ready with the brandy.

The older girls were getting a bit beyond sharing their life with a selection of wandering reptiles and I knew that sooner or later I would have a very serious rebellion on my hands.

It almost reached a crisis when a twin, now grown and lovely, and very prone to spending hours in the bathroom, locked herself in for one of her marathons. Not for long on this occasion though. She very soon came screaming back through the door and I just managed to gather, as she fled at speed to the refuge of her bedroom, that one of the husband's little wanderers was coiled up under the towel in the bath. "Naughty little thing!!!" I must say though, it does give you a start coming face to face with a snake in unexpected circumstances.

With the sun streaming through my kitchen window, I was enjoying gazing at the garden and the fields beyond over the low curtain. I was considering what a blessing it was to be able to look out at the sheep and the flowing hay fields, right to the ribbon of sea in the distance. A tiny flicker of movement and my eyes focused quickly onto the top of the curtain about nose level. There we were eye to eye and much too close for comfort. The grass snake had spread himself out in the sun in comfort and must have had his eye on me from quite some time. It was almost get rid of them time!

The fields and streams of freedom were beckoning our pets.

There was an addition made on one occasion, quite by accident, and this time I was shocked rigid and will be eternally grateful that no dire calamity took place.

My eldest son then about ten proudly brought home a specimen of large proportions and interesting disposition, having taken a bite at the glove of his cousin - I was shown the fang marks. The boys had popped the newcomer into the large glass tank with the rest of the occupants and they went off to tell Dad. "You'll be pleased when you see it Dad. It's the biggest grass snake of them all". Big it certainly was. Grass snake it certainly was not. A full grown and angry adder and to be fished out of the tank with two-foot long Victorian tongs and secured in an escape-proof box. Then the husband had to trek across fields and marshland to let it loose in as secluded a spot as possible. I've no doubt the poor chap was thoroughly sick and tired of human interference and delighted to be away, but his delight would not have compared with my relief at seeing the back of him.

It wasn't long after we set our pets free in a quiet and lovely spot in springtime, so they could live out their lives as nature intended, and for that matter, so could I.

Throw Me An Apple

Sheba the Alsatian was an animal of many parts, acquired originally for the purpose of family protection, she soon showed her mettle. At first sign of a raised male voice, she disappeared up the stairs and under the nearest bed, where her nerves completely gave away. I was pleased she only proved incontinent under stress, Alsatians are not small dogs.

Sheba ate strange things, and I was astonished when my missing silk scarf re-appeared almost a week later streaming across a field behind her.

Her presence was generally enough to affect an atmosphere of security but she continually let us down. She was accidentally left alone in the lounge with a gentleman making some business enquiries. When I returned, Sheba had her "I've been stupid again" expression and the gentleman was putting himself out to be ultra-polite. I found out why when the man had gone and I closed the lounge curtains. Behind the sofa was a regular lake of vomit.

Amongst Sheba's endearing traits was her affinity for water. Any water, but wherever possible, putrid water. A Sunday stroll ended in disaster. The children in their going to tea clothes, because that's where they were going. The Alsatian needing a little exercise, and a muddy stream. We did our best to keep her out of the mud pit, but we were too late, plan number one having failed, we did our best to keep her out of the car. We rushed the kids in before she actually noticed and almost got the door closed and windows sealed but not quite: Sheba in a fit of panic flew to the car and forced her way through a closing door in a frenzy of insecurity, kissing us all in her ecstasy of being reunited with her loved ones. We were smothered with love, saliva and other things. A pathologist would have had a field day analysing the contents of our car on this occasion.

Another dog with whom we had a short acquaintance was Lucy, a rag-bag with cross eyes, a real untrainable ragamuffin, who really blotted her copy book when on a walk she encountered a three legged dog, half her size and proceeded to harass him unmercifully, snapping deliberately at where the fourth leg should have been, and creating no end of fuss. A youthful visitor came home to me with tales of this grossly wicked and unjustified behaviour. "You can't blame Lucy dear, she can't count", was all I could say in her defence.

Pebbles the red setter was inclined to bolting, she could cover many miles whilst you gave chase and be home again four hours before you, waiting to greet you with tail wagging and tongue lolling. Sadly, we had to part company when she took a liking for the local sheep flock, but when I met her new owners several years later, they told me she was still going strong and they had loved her every minute. Before she left us, she certainly put is through our paces, especially the husband. He was the one in hot pursuit more often than not.

Once the route took him through a housing estate, through endless back gardens. He had to watch helplessly as she leapt six foot high fences. Helpful householders rushed out with bowls of water for her to drink, balls for her to play with etc. but just as you were within a whisper of catching her, off she would go again.

Finally, she disappeared without trace amidst the houses and a few moments went by. Eventually she re-appeared, being led by the collar by a large gent. He looked at my husband and said: "Is this yours?" Pebbles had rushed into his house and found him eating dinner. Being a dog to whom food was everything, she had seated herself beside him, panting, drooling and gazing into his plate.

Throw Me An Apple

Pebbles attended obedience lessons with her constant companion, one of the twins, and learned absolutely nothing. I often watched them disappear down the road together for these sessions, both beautiful, their hair shining in the sun, both with their heads in the air and a distinctive rebellious streak. This twin shared the big brass bed with one of her younger sisters and when I peered in to say good night, I often smiled to myself at the sight of three sleeping heads on the pillows, the two girls and Pebbles in the middle. Both girls sound asleep and a red setter waiting apprehensively to be discovered and turfed out, one eye open. Pebbles loved this twin so much. She chewed and ate everything remotely connected with her. A mixed blessing.

A calamitous day for one and all was thrust upon us one wet October when my poor sister-in-law accidentally let Pebbles out during the peak of her fanaticism with the local farmer's sheep. I was very pregnant and out of the chase altogether and the husband and his sister gave chase. Over a barbed wire fence they went and into the mire of the sheep field. I couldn't watch the interim goings on, but went to meet them when I knew the deed was done. The deed was done indeed. I have never seen such mud. My sister in-law was totally covered to past her knees and spattered from there up. The husband who was still making his way back to the lane, holding the dog by the collar in one hand and one of his shoes with the other, was just beyond the beyond. I began to laugh and my sister-in-law quickly stopped me. "He's really mad", she said and nothing more. I didn't laugh, at least not until I asked why he wasn't wearing both shoes. It was obvious really. He had leaped for the dog at one stage and missed. It was so awful, and it was everywhere. The only one who looked happy was Pebbles. She'd had a whale of a time.

The chickens were lovable and so were the three Aylesbury ducks, and if it were possible, I would have a garden full of them. I can only remember one regrettable act to do with the ducks and it wasn't anything to do with them really. It was the husband. The small garden pond that housed generations of frogs had for some reason become rather devoid of duck weed and didn't look so good, so an expedition was decided upon.

It was a very hot afternoon, so a really happy event was anticipated as we took off across open fields, heading for a STREAM. We reached a point on the bank of the stream where a huge drainage pipe was making access to the water easier. The water was clear and the weed was abundant. The sun was shining, the bees droned, pollen made a haze all around us and happiness and peace settled on all of us unpursued.
"How shall we get it?" enquired the husband.
"Can you reach it from here?"
"No".
"What if I hang onto the back of your trousers?"
"Yes, that should do it".

It did it alright. It did it very well. The husband reaching at full stretch across the drainage pipe had a good bucketful of duck weed and was just reaching for the last little bit when his trouser button suddenly parted company with his trousers and in the name of decency, I let go of the trousers and the husband.

It was like the launching of some ocean going vessel down a slipway. It was almost graceful. I apologised profusely as he sank into the water, then disappeared into the thick mud beyond. I smiled sweetly and hopefully as he surfaced and enquired how he was faring. He told me how slippery the mud was and how deep it was, and disappeared again. He finally found his feet and went to make his way out.

"I think you've lost all the weed dear, and really, as you are

actually on the spot now, do you think you could, er, um, er, well er"....
I could have sworn he snarled, but it did make sense and he later emerged victorious with a good pot full of weed.

He was my hero, but he really stank and we didn't dare consider what came from that drainage pipe, but flies followed us all the way home. He had no choice but to strip on the back door step and dash into the shower whilst I dealt with the clothing, having first ceremoniously put every scrap of that valuable and hard come by weed into our pond. It looked lovely, so natural and I was sure the baby frogs would appreciate the cover it gave from the possibility of marauding enemies.

The husband re-appeared shortly, smelling sweet and looking good, and what was even more important, he was still in love with me, at least for the next few moments.

We went to inspect the crowning glory of our endeavours. Hand in hand we strolled across the lawn, along the crazy paving and peered into the depths of our pond (the converted ex-bath tub).
"I thought you said you'd put it in?"
"I did, I did".
"Well, where is it?"

Silence whilst we considered the mystery. We knew the stuff didn't melt. A slight rustle in a small shrub drew our attention to an Aylesbury duck. Duck weed on her chest, duck weed in her beak. DUCK WEED.

Pussy cats of all shapes, sizes, and shades have allowed us to share their lives over the years. There have been the hearth loving variety, the Mum and Dad teams who have presented us with batches of adorable kittens, the slightly wild and distant type who honoured us with their presence for a short time on cold winter evenings, then returned to their true calling, across the fields and under the hedgerows.

They have brought us numerous gifts, proudly heralding their arrival with a yowl or a meow, or wrapping themselves affectionately round our legs whilst we cringed as tactfully as possible and removed the remains or complete object at the earliest possible opportunity.

One rather more refined feline presented us with live gifts. They would arrive in the hallway and scamper straight into the lounge to take refuge in the fireplace. The great blocks of sandstone and numerous copper and brass items surrounding it offered ample cover, and as we all thought, they were the cutest things on four paws, the field mice with their lovely furry scuttling bodies and giant beady eyes dwelt securely with us for a few days before we popped them back home.

They specially seemed to enjoy sitting under the copper kettle or tunnelling along the brass fender. The log pile too was a firm favourite, but a corner on the floor under the bookcase was one little visitor's favourite abode and he proceeded to make it very cosy for himself. This one stayed a little longer than most and every evening around seven he would come out of his chosen abode and entertain us for a little while running across the carpet, gathering items of food, crumbs etc. that we had left discreetly for this very purpose.

We were the audience, he was the cabaret, and we liked it that way. Our nightly floor show quite slipped our minds as we sat chatting after tea to our guest. First the rustling under the bookcase, my cue to panic, then the nudges and glances from the children, they couldn't wait for the uproar to start. The dear ladies sitting contentedly, sipping their drinks. I just couldn't let it happen to them. More rustling, louder now and noticeable.

"What's that dear?"

Children in fits of giggles, also falling about in anticipation.

"It must be later than I thought!" I announce. "They're obviously overtired".

I growl at the kids. "Past their bedtime probably!"

I rise to my feet and stamp around the bookcase. That should hold him for a little while! For once it did, and as the guests leave, our friend appears, and my reputation is saved this time.

Raffles, last in line of a regiment of pets, reigns supreme in my home and deals with us as he sees fit. A Siamese with a loud voice, very little sense of balance, an over-rated sense of justice and a determination to sit on your lap regardless of what crisis or commitment is afoot, but always with his back to you, to keep his dignity.

We dare not leave him out when we go to bed because he has the whole street up with the sound of his demands to come in. Our home is open house to his acquaintances, they are frequently invited to lunch and he sits watching whilst we try to explain to them that it's bad manners to just invite oneself without permission of the landlord. Same with a would-be boarder one night. I had quite a conversation with a large tabby sitting half in and half out of my bedroom window one night. I told him that I didn't know of any arrangements having been made for him to sleep, and it would be as well if he would have the decency to use the back door in future. Raffles just looked on, without as much as twitching a whisker.

Throw Me An Apple

I've seen his sophisticated and cool image wear a bit thin on occasion. I've seen him watching birds from under the garden table, with rising excitement and anticipation, and I've watched as he's leapt for one, completely forgetting that he is still under the table and come staggering out, trying to work out how the table did that.

Fence walking has never been his strong point either. I've watched him parading up and down the fence for the benefit of the neighbours and losing his footing and his dignity frequently.

The peak of his performance came one night when I called him home. I heard him climb the fence, then I heard a frenzied scraping and scratching, then an almighty "splash". A few short seconds later the aristocrat shot into the house having shrunk to half his size and covered in duck weed. Then came the indignities of a bath, he wouldn't look at me for days.

This cat owns his own chair, but I didn't know that. I thought it was mine, consequently, I thought I was quite at liberty to move it around the house at will, and proceeded to do so. I should have realized the great old armchair in the lounge was no longer mine. He was always sprawled across it surrounded by cushions, or draped across the back of it, catching the sunlight, or raking at it unmercifully in an ecstasy of claw sharpening. The real clue came, I suppose, when we sat on that chair and the blue eyes flushed and blazed in indignation as we squeezed our way into his domain. I was at last left in no doubt when the chair finally, to my estimation, was past its best and due to be pensioned off. I moved it out of the lounge and got as far as the kitchen. Raffles had been hopping and leaping about, yowling and generally throwing a tantrum. None of this had conveyed anything to me so far. Finally, his last ditch effort came. He clung onto the side of that old chair and either lashed out

Christine Wright

Throw Me An Apple

with his paw full of noodles or snarled and bit anyone who came anywhere near his pride and joy. I gave in under the pressure, found an old loose cover to hide the devastation beneath and the chair travelled no further than the kitchen. My gross ignorance was finally forgiven, and we all settled back to normality!!!

Raffles was extremely proud of the first mouse caught. In it came for the old ritual of presenting the carnage, out it went to a hail of yowling and indignant objections. Much to our horror, it was continually resurrected and we went through the dreadful rigmarole of chasing Raffles, retrieving the corpse and throwing it as far as possible. It was never far enough, and the final straw came a fortnight later when we caught him sneakily burying it under the kitchen rug. Horrible. Horrible. This time we did something a bit more permanent, the first mouse to have a "decent burial".

We claimed some notoriety for wild bird rescue and in spring, quite a few fledglings came our way. We didn't have a very high success rate, but we did our best and the garden was well dug in all weathers and at all times of the day as our charges were always fed on demand.

One particular little ball of feather and down left his mark, however. This one was a bit bigger than most and he seemed to have real determination.

Beginning his stay in a cage for protection from our pussies, he very soon grew strong and vigorous and had to be given the run of the lounge. Progressing quickly from being fed by tweezers to pecking his own worms from a container full of soil, he was flying from lampshade to sideboard etc.

Our whole family was disrupted, the lounge was out of bounds to all and the cleaning was a constant job, and for what? This little half-grown blackbird really thought I was his Mum and I was absolutely delighted.

I can only remember him letting me down once and that was when the husband's friend and his family came to tea. The husband's friend had brought with him an electric car track on the pretext that it would amuse the children. The fact that the children weren't the slightest bit interested didn't seem to bother them too much - in fact, I think they were far too engrossed themselves to even notice.

Of course, the only room large enough was the lounge so I explained about our feathered guest, who by then was a confident flier and quite an acrobat with it, his favourite perch being the lampshade which actually served a dual role due to its shape. It was round with cylinder effect down the centre where the bulb hung and was covered in raffia so it was easy to cling to. The hole down the centre seemed to remind our feathered friend of the edge of the nest, as whenever he perched there, he seemed to splurge straight through it. Naturally, we kept clear of that spot, and I did actually explain to the husband's friend, in as dignified way as I could about the situation, assuring him that it was extremely temporary and not using the word "splurge".

I watched the construction of the track and reminded them periodically of the impending dangers, but the track spread itself right through the danger zone and so did the guest. All of a sudden it happened, and "splat" it was a direct hit.

So there it all was, chickens that perched on the window sill and came in through the open window because we let them and they liked it, a snake that disappeared and was found peeping out of the back of an old radio, a toad named Albert who graced our garden on Summer evenings, frogs by the score, a lizard that could bite so hard it could dent your fingernail, a rabbit that thought it was a cat and refused to live out of doors, numerous birds, mice, pussy cats, dogs, hamsters, gerbils that seemed to live forever and so on and so on, and probably tons more I never found out about, sneaked in in people's pockets and out in carrier bags. One of my biggest dreads was emptying the boys' pockets before I washed their clothes.

Christine Wright

Visitors

Guests have come and guests have gone, some have returned and others have disappeared without trace. Most who return like to sit and relate their experience of past visits, some have done this at the most inappropriate time, and in the company of quite unappreciative audiences. It has been rather difficult to be diplomatic on occasion.

Without exception, all our staying guests, both new and old, regardless of economic background or education or breeding, have to understand that fitting into the family arrangement and environment is a task they have to be willing to undertake.

We have been long past putting on airs and graces many decades ago. We still manage the clean linen and long walks to wear them all out though, and the stalwarts are still returning.

One such determined young man attached himself to the family initially and briefly, through one of my girls, but stayed on to encompass one and all. This one at the outset had no idea of the volume of children and animals he was to encounter when he accepted our invitation of "you must come down and meet us all". I must add here, that at this stage in our history, we lived in a property converted from two to one house, the only way we could find at the time of accommodating such a large household. Consequently, there were two of everything in the way of bathrooms, toilets, kitchens and lounges, and it could get a bit confusing, particularly as one bathroom was used as anything but a bathroom.

The first thing that became apparent about this young man

Throw Me An Apple

was his impeccable manners and good breeding, together with an earnest desire not only to fit in, but not to put us under any pressure. This became abundantly clear on his very first morning.

I thought I was early out of bed, but he was down first, also the youngest member of the family, about two years old at the time. It was a pleasant sight, sunny kitchen, guest sitting relaxed and content with the world, drinking very strong coffee and chatting to infant, who was munching a carrot.

Infant was remarkably quiet and also washed and orderly.. I suppose instinct should have told me something wasn't quite average, but it really was very early. After the preliminaries. "Good morning, did you sleep well?" etc., my next enquiry was about the carrot. "Oh, don't worry, I washed him first", interrupted the determined to be laid back guest. "Oh, thank you very much, that was very thoughtful of you", I said, in absolute innocence. The guest smiled. "Can I make you a drink?" he said. I thought, "what a lovely young man, he can definitely come again". "I'll just pop upstairs and sort out the sprogs (other children). I'll be back in about five minutes for my drink".

As I mounted the stairs, the most atrocious smell made itself apparent. It got worse, and I was led straight to infant's room. Dreadful negative thoughts had built up with every step nearer his door. Embarrassment of the most intense and worse nature was creeping over me as my suspicions gradually became founded on raw facts. The absolute worst possible thing had happened, and when I opened his bedroom door, the stark reality and immensity of the whole dreadful situation really exploded in front of me. It was obviously not infant's fault. I had actually never before seen so much, so well distributed and desperately obnoxious in all my time. I closed the bedroom door and staggered back to the kitchen wondering how I could ever face this young gentleman again. How on earth had he managed to strip and bath infant in that state? He'd never had anything to do with tiny tots as far as I knew, and certainly nothing to do with vast quantities of what lurked behind that bedroom door.

I poked my head round the kitchen door and tried to smile. Nonchalance was out of the question, this was the pits. He managed to smile quite freely. "I'm ever so sorry", I gasped. "I've never seen anything quite that awful", I said, and fell silent. "I'm sorry I couldn't manage to tackle it" he said. "I'm afraid it was beyond me". "How on earth did you manage him?" I asked incredulously. "Well, that was essential. He was determined to come into my room to see me and chatted away quite oblivious to his condition, I suppose I was resigned to the inevitable". We both laughed, and I knew from that moment on, that if this guest came back, he would be a very permanent feature in our lives for many years to come, and one of our dearest friends. He is.

We also found that there was just one more little facet to this tale. Years later he added, in the rush to deal with infant that day, he hastily parcelled him into one of the bathrooms only to encounter guests already installed. Three baby ducks, too young to be safe in the garden, had been given temporary residence there. Common sense we thought, but gross eccentricity to a city-dwelling young chap encountering such things for the first time. I think his must have been one of the most gross and colourful initiations of any guests we had ever beguiled into "coming to meet the family".

He's often visited us over the years, and by some twist of fate, was often "with us" at crisis times, of which there have been a rather substantial quantity. Some very bumpy and choppy times have been floated over with him in tow, as

Christine Wright

Throw Me An Apple

anchor.

Things happen in our household whether guests are present or not, life just rolls on relentlessly. We do our best to present a civilised front, but which do people really prefer, I wondered, the veneer, or the solid oak? We generally end up revealing the solid oak, albeit a bit knotty on occasion. Perhaps stripped pine may be better analogy.

Animals have frequently been the instruments of laying bare the truth of the situation quite innocently of course, but sometimes I did rather suspect their innocence. Take "Chelsea" for instance. A brilliant mouser, but something of a showman too, judging from his determination to go about his business only when visitors arrived and primarily during those confusing and harassing few moments as they walked through the front door and were having their coats taken, being questioned as to tea or coffee, and being urged to go into the living room.

Once marooned in the hallway, Chelsea would subject them to one of his most flamboyant displays of catch the rodent. The scene would be set for impending chaos and possible hysterical outbursts, not to say the complete destruction of our family name. I would then begin my routine of "effervescence if it kills me", and leap about bubbling and smiling, ushering - to the point of shoving bodily - guests into the lounge, all the time pretending nothing of a murderous nature was taking place in our civilised and cosy home and totally ignoring the astonished guests' mumbled questions. "What's your cat doing? Did you see what that cat had in its claws? Was that a rodent running into her kitchen, dear?" I settled for "have a nice cup of tea and relax, my dears. I'll be with you in a minute", whereupon I fled the lounge and proceeded to chastise the proud and positively bristling Chelsea and remove the evidence of his latest conquest.

Cats have been a source of distress for a few of our visitors over the years, not that any of it was intentional of course, like the other distinguished guest who was obliged to flee prematurely from the lavatory, having been in the direct path of two of our current feline residents making an extremely hasty return home, through the open window just above where he was seated. I'm still undecided as to who suffered the severest shock - they or he.

There was also the "Cuddles" incident which rather inconveniently took place during the preparation of ham and salad rolls, fish-paste sandwiches, (with cress of course) and fancy cakes for tea, not overlooking slapping the cream on the trifle, in fact, we were about at that stage, my close friend and I, when number five, then about three, came strolling into the kitchen. Just developing a sense of humour, she looked up at me, smiled and said, "I think Cuddles is eating the canary". With that familiar sinking feeling creeping over me I replied, "that's not a very nice joke, my dear, don't say horrible things". (One can always hope in these situations). The reply, "well, I still think Cuddles is eating the canary". A second to face reality and I shot into the lounge, followed by the close friend, a little too close for my liking on this unfortunate occasion. Of course, Cuddles was eating the canary. For some reason, no one seemed to fancy the fish-paste!!!

My children too have had their moments of abandon. Having chickens out the back served many purposes, the primary one being an abundance of lovely eggs, and apart from many others, I really liked them.

Our house was designed with two stairways leading up opposite ends of the house, and one could go up one side, right across the top floor and down the other in an unbroken circle for as long as you wished, round and round and round. I might add, the tiny tots often did this route until captured at the bottom in the hallway and redirected into activities of a more constructive nature. All these seemingly unrelated features came together one summer's evening and the results were as usual catastrophically unsettling and the catalyst in this case was a mere egg.

One of the twins, now grown, beautiful, sophisticated and very appearance conscious, in a moment of uncontrolled abandon, lobbed an egg at their brother. Her brother, also in his teens, nimble, alert and an exceptionally good shot, merely ducked and arranged to retaliate. The scene was set, the affair which began in the garden, gained access to the house, visitors took their positions to witness the whole event, and the drama swung into action. The sophisticated young lady ran screaming through the house with irate brother in hot pursuit, the egg the real villain of the piece, took flight, and without falling in its commitment, met its mark, namely the right side of the beautiful head of our sophisticated young lady.

Just for a moment here, consider an egg. Innocent, average, common, uncomplicated, nourishing (even for hair) - but only when fresh. When this same object is for some obscure reason at least eighteen months old, well, that's when severe and terrible complications set in. It is at this precise second when our sophisticated, unflappable, young lady totally freaks out. The stench was beyond the realms of belief. The appearance was positively gruesome but the stench - that was the truly agonizing thing. That that obnoxious and ghastly mass of putrefaction could be actually smeared and clinging to that beautiful pampered head was almost sacrilegious. The poor girl ran totally out of control, round and round the house to the point when we were all certain she would very soon be in orbit. In her wake the whole house was becoming a vast stink bomb. What could possibly be done to stem the flow of this calamity?

Christine Wright

Someone held open the shower-room door, and waited opposite it at the bottom of the stairs to grab her in mid-flight. Hysterical screaming heralded her descent into my arms. A brief struggle ensued whilst she was bundled into the shower-room, clothes being torn off as fast as humanly possible. I truly love the girl but I could only suffer her aromatic presence for a matter of seconds. She was in the shower for what seemed a decade. As for her brother, launcher of the missile of devastation, he had disappeared as soon as the screaming started. He always did have a way of sensing when things were about to get right out of hand. The visitors? Well. Another end to a perfect day I'd say.

I didn't know our visitors personally at the outset of their stay. This was mainly due to the size of the family, the older children being free to invite whoever they wished, provided they undertook to entertain, cater and provide a spot for them to lay their heads. Often a "spot" was the only available area of space left. Many a morning I have staggered down one flight of stairs to greet the day in as lonely, civilised and peaceful a way as possible, to find a total stranger doing the very same down the opposite flight. The conversation frequently went as follows, in a semi whisper: "Who are you?" Name followed, then "Who are you, then?" "I live here dear, what about you?" "Oh, I'm so-and-so's friend." "I see. Are you staying long?" "I am not sure" "I see. We'd better have a cup of coffee." I never panicked; I knew I had the ultimate weapon should I need it. I rarely had to set the kids on unwanted guests. Later, should the need arise, they always came through, bless 'em.

The same rule applied very often. We acquired some very close friends from these obscure and embarrassed individuals, some have travelled many miles away, and months may go by but sooner or later we are re-united, and more colour is splashed into our life.

When visitors return, we often lapse into nostalgia and when friends meet other friends, stories are swapped and passed to and fro like trays of sweets. Most are fun, memorable and palatable enough. It's just the odd one or two that stick in your throat.

One such tale confounded guests on two occasions and I suffered a double flush of embarrassment. It revolved around a meal time, always a dodgy time at best. Time was short and the children, especially number four, aged about three, were being so slow with their meal, I had to hurry them up as several visitors were about to expire from lack of food. It has been at least eight hours since toast was served!!! Ten minutes later and number four was still on her beans. "Look dear, if you don't get a move on, I'll have to ram it down your throat". Now what a child psychologist would have made with an expression like that, I can't imagine.

What an unpleasant prospect, I regretted the momentary lapse of tact and understanding immediately, but not as much as I regretted it later on and for subsequent visits of these friends. I returned to the lounge and guests and sat down. Two minutes later number four appeared at the living room door. A Snow White look-alike with a bowl of beans. "What is it dear?" A big smile, a flattering of eyelashes and "will you ram it down my throat please Mummy like you said you would." I sat there silently, swallowed up with remorse. The guests, however, found the whole thing positively hilarious and fell about till dinner was served later on, and now I relive the whole scenario when our friends return and begin, "Hey, do you remember your face that day etc., etc., etc."

Another little trip down memory lane frequently rears its ugly head. After a day at the beach many years ago, and a certain pair of cut-down jeans worn by the husband, and held together by two safety pins directly underneath. There was no time for a needle and thread job that morning. It was quite a rough day for the beach really, giant waves and gale force winds, but that was no deterrent. There were crowds of us too, all our visitors and all of my sister-in-law's family (my husband's sister) plus several more who had tagged on. Who would be first into the sea? Off went the husband, hopping in the shallows, cut-down jeans, plus safety pins still intact - then the giant wave. On it came, swept the husband off his feet and threw him back almost onto the shingle, he was fine, but what had that wave done with those safety pins, lost without trace and the remainder of the cut-down jeans flapping wildly in the gale. As usual, in a crisis, I was frozen and useless; thank goodness my sister-in-law came to the rescue with her quick-thinking and large bath towel. The husband's honour was saved, everyone could open their eyes again, and the whole story went down in the archives, to be resurrected whenever it could cause as much embarrassment as possible, and believe me, it has. It has been related at some very inappropriate times and before some blushing disapproving ladies.

A courting couple, very much in love, and determined to stay in very close proximity of each other used to visit us frequently, some years ago. The young man had to be particularly determined as he was not the only male in our household besotted with that young lady. Our eldest son, then around five years old, was his adamant rival for her affections. Wherever they were, he appeared, and whenever they sat on the sofa, up he popped between them, whereupon, he never failed to kiss her arm from fingertips to shoulder and whisper sweet-nothings in her ear. The one who suffered from all this intensity in the end was the poor old sofa.

The young couple appeared through the living room door one day, having just managed to dodge his arch rival, he grabbed his intended and both flung themselves onto the sofa as far up one end as possible. I watched on as the sofa completely gave way leaving the astonished couple hovering for a split second in mid-air, then coming down in a tangle of arms and legs, embarrassment and injured pride. It seemed the cards were stacked against them.

Christine Wright

Cars

Ambivalent could well describe our feelings toward the cavalcade of motor vehicles that have accompanied us over the years. There were times when I would much rather they wouldn't bother accompanying us, for all the use they were.

My first car was so temperamental I was sure it should have made a career in amateur dramatics and go off and leave us all in peace. The children spent more time pushing it than riding in it and it was always that one last push that seemed to do more harm than good, particularly one day on their way to school. "Just one more push should do it my dears?!" And so it did, but left four children face down in a large puddle as it roared off in triumph. Was that the plugs misfiring or a suppressed chuckle? This old contemptible finally went out in a blaze of glory about thirty miles from our destination. Smoke poured from the dashboard and I abandoned it at great speed, completely neglecting to inform the passengers who were looking out the back window thinking something had dropped off. I flew back to give them strict instructions to vacate. I had no choice really, my handbag was still in the car and the ignition was still on.

Various items have parted company with our vehicles in transit on occasion. A back door on one car gave the kids a very nasty surprise as it decided it had travelled with us far enough, but we had to restrain it a little longer as we had only had the wretched car a few weeks, so the most capable and trustworthy child in the back clung on for dear life until we reached a garage. The wandering item was welded on securely and so was its opposite counterpart. I must add, they looked positively ridiculous, but we stuck on our blinkers and continued on our way.

Throw Me An Apple

"ONE EMERGED FROM A BARN

Those doors came to have quite an effective use actually. The twins, now adolescent and inclined occasionally to the odd emotional outburst, usually accompanied by what is often described as some "lip" and occurring quite frequently around breakfast time, before leaving for school, would then expect a lift. Naturally, I would bear no resentment and off we would go, but instead of parking a discreet distance from the school where the offensive doors could do no damage to their adolescent pride, I would insist on parking right outside the school gates where hordes of curious peers would have a field-day as our young ladies struggled to make their rather unrefined exits over the back of the front passenger seat and out the front door.

The husband, purchaser of our vehicles and recipient of no end of ribbing when he proudly turned up with his acquisitions, this guy was gifted with the ability to root out and track down some of the most clapped out specimens struggling around our roads. One emerged from a barn and the proud owner - a farming gentleman - suffered the wrench of losing it bravely and quite possibly did a jig as our hero drove it off. The steering was exceptionally heavy and we finally found out why. About to leave a friend's home, the prospect of battling through a three point turn was not a rosy one, so I cut a corner. Carefully mounting the pavement with the back right hand wheel, we prepared to take off. It was at that precise moment we parted company with the front right hand wheel and the strangest sinking sensation I've experienced in a vehicle followed. I glanced up the hill, to the left, and looked at the husband. Then we did what was the customary thing with us. We phoned a scrapyard, gathered our belongings and walked home.

Motorways seem to have brought out the worst in our cars occasionally. One specimen that could only be described as mutton dressed as lamb, had us completely led up the garden path. This one looked good, plush carpet, clock when cars didn't have clocks and a healthy appetite for oil!! So sure was I of the capabilities of this vehicle that I insisted on my brother, his wife and children and luggage accompanying me, three of my children and my luggage, one hundred and fifty miles to his home, despite the fact he had rail tickets, which would have seen them all safely home and dry. We took off. It was a glorious day and it came to an end in a blaze of glory when the big end went on the M1. Apologies have never been more inadequate, a speech was out of the question, excuses would have been totally out of order, and silence pervaded for quite some time. We were towed so far, given a lift, caught a bus, then a train, then another bus! The husband, who had left by train to meet us at my brother's home, had arrived many hours before. Having gone through the various stages of anxiety, worry and boredom, he had finally gone off to inspect the local architecture and had found the local pub a specimen of great historical interest.

Our latest and most acceptable car has been an exception to our general rule, but just to keep up the tradition, it shed its exhaust on a motorway when we were returning from holiday. Not what you'd call too much of a hassle by general standards, that is, not until you suddenly become aware that you are absolutely desperate to use the loo. There is always a complication. Not a hedge or reasonable sized bush for miles and no sign of the rescue van. After some serious consideration, you find the answer is somewhere in the realms of grin and bear it, but I'm afraid the grinning soon stops. Finally, in desperation, a decision is made.

If you were to change clothes, from trousers to flowing skirt you might just manage to create enough camouflage to make relief possible. That, coupled with the fact the cars travel so fast, and those tiny bushes seem to have grown at least a foot in these last two hours. This could be it. No sooner said than done. That's the skirt on. "Stay put, Muv,

Christine Wright

the rescue has just arrived". "You are not serious". "Hello Madam, what's the trouble?" "Well, it's a long story, how far is the nearest garage, my dear?". You're left not being able to decide whether his appearance is a blessing or a curse.

Travelling to the Midlands in a positive eye-sore of a car, we hit slow traffic in London. My eldest daughter was in the back with her husband and our youngest tot. The husband was driving, he'd bought the thing, so that was the least he could do, it was one of his star purchases. It turned out it was just as well it was a heap. It was hot sunny day with an occasional tiny bit of breeze, and for some reason none of us had a window open, apart from a two inch slit on my husband's side. It was as well, I can tell you, because an extraordinary thing happened. The traffic was hardly moving and we sat and watched oncoming cars. A sort of low loader type small lorry was on its way towards us and it was heaped high to overflowing with some sort of sludge. I was watching it all the way up, wondering where it could possibly have been dredged from. It really wasn't what I would have expected to see, being transported through city streets. It would have been more at home on a pig farm or maybe a cesspit even. The colour and consistency for some reason grabbed my attention too. It was a combination of dark green, black, grey and brown. It didn't actually run, but seemed to ooze a little and was distinctly lumpy in parts. Most peculiar.

As it got closer and closer, ever so slowly, I gazed and wondered. As it drew almost opposite our car, it had to make a very sudden and jerky stop. At that very second, a tiny gust of wind skimmed off a goodly dollop of the contents of the lorry and sent it hurtling at our car. There must have been a good dustbin full in all, and I watched it flying through the air in horror. No one else seemed to have been taking note, but when it all landed, they certainly did. For a start, it was instant blackout and I yelled to the husband to put the

Throw Me An Apple

brakes on, as he hadn't, and we couldn't see a thing. Being in so much traffic and not being able to see outside the car left us in more than a predicament. Also, what was now oozing in curdled masses all over the car would have come oozing into it if we opened the doors.

I just couldn't believe what was taking place. It was just too ridiculous to be real. Seconds in steamy silence ticked by and the smell started to creep in through the vents. All I can say is: it was pretty grim, and not likely to encourage the appetite in any way. As we were trapped, but couldn't just sit there either, something had to be done. The idea of going outside with a bit of tissue was turned down because nobody would volunteer, so we just sat in the dark a bit longer. Giggling had by now commenced and was reaching hysterical proportions. At this point, the husband boldly announced "he was going out there". "Wait," I said, "try the wipers". By some miracle, it worked. Slowly at first, sludge flew in all directions, and we finally had enough vision to proceed. On closer inspection a few miles further on, we found it was completely covering the roof. It was right down the driver's side. It was smothered over the bonnet and up the front, one third covering the passenger side and splattered over the boot. The only saving grace was it hadn't come in the window, but the smell did and continued to plague us all the way to the Midlands, gradually diminishing as it dried in the wind and caked up.

Other drivers we passed were amazed to say the least and it was a source of great hilarity as we watched their looks and expressions of disbelief. The funniest expressions of all though, came from the lorry and bus drivers who drew up beside our dishevelled and stinking vehicle and had a clear bird's eye view of the whole spectacle.

Another small irony was the fact that my eldest daughter travelling with us, was by nature scrupulously clean to the point of being obsessed with things that surrounded her being totally spotless and sweet smelling at all times, and under all circumstances. To have to sit in that travelling quagmire must have tested her every nerve, but really it was all so bizarre and totally unreal that I rather suspect she may have withdrawn into a dream world for the duration of the journey. If she had, she would have found me there.

Once the car was actually equipped with its own foot spa. A piece of household equipment we would never under normal circumstance have paid good money for, but as it came free with the car, we found we had to put up with it. We discovered it not long after the car was purchased, on the first wet day in fact. We thought we'd take the car to save getting our feet wet but as it worked out, when we drove through the first puddle of more than three inches depth, we found we had our very own private spurting, squirting, bubbling foot, shin and thigh spa.

The funniest bit was the way it had been fitted, to actually squirt jets of water up the trouser leg of the driver. There was another more serious problem than the water though. It was that the fumes came in when the water did not. We didn't realise at first, but just accepted the fuzzy head feeling that coincided with our journeys and put it down to our increasing age. Eventually, however, we took a ride out to a café with my daughter and her husband and stopped the car outside. We were discussing what we would have one minute, and sometime later woke up to find we had all fallen asleep. Very strange. We're not that old!! We concluded fumes were coming in and it was later confirmed. We were relieved that dozing off outside cafés was not to become the highlight of our social activity.

Christine Wright

You gave me some of my sunniest days

One thing I think I would recommend above most things, is that if possible, try to arrange that your in-laws are your friends before they are your in-laws. I stumbled upon this gem of philosophy quite by accident.

One day, in a crowd of acquaintances, I looked up and spotted a beaming smile, twinkling blue eyes and an explosion of happiness all wrapped up in a person. It took me a split second to realise that this girls was going to be special, and a friendship of a very precious and valuable nature had been born in the burst of a single smile.

Since then, we have shared food and clothes, thoughts and opinions, homes, furniture, sunshine, gardens, friends and sometimes children, many, many things, and the most precious thing she shared with me was her brother.

Our children have, to a very large degree, grown up together - they are all of similar ages. We both agreed that for our children outside was the place to be, so with loaded prams, we would take off into the country or off to the sea for our free and easy, and fresh air filled days.

At one time, she lived five miles away from me, so we would arrange our days to meet half way, and then either wander through the country lanes or return to her house or mine. Our babies grew up on sunshine, fresh fruit, freedom to run through grass, throw leaves, stroke sheep and animals, pick flowers, splash the great ocean, feel stones and trees and snow and love, watch the clouds, storms and little birds and drink their fill of Mother's milk and peace and contended security.

I remember a beautiful frosty winter's day when we gathered

Throw Me An Apple

round a great bonfire with the babies and children. Trees had been felled locally and the fire was warm and bright. For years later, our husbands had to put up with great chunks of tree trunk in the lounge of our homes, having pride of place, whilst we contemplated how long it had taken for our pieces of tree to grow. I must add here, not all creatures appreciate the value of such things. A friend's dog of obvious low intellect and multiple breeding, led solely by its baser instincts, quite mistook my table for a common tree trunk and had to be hastily removed and severely reprimanded for its lack of self-control, albeit in confusing circumstances.

Another of our heart's desire was to own an old brass bed, and for years we bided our time and hoped one day our opportunity would come. Mine came first and for eight pounds worth of brass and iron double bedstead, less two bed knobs, my happiness was bubbling out of my ears. The thrill of sleeping in a great big old bed like that, it was wonderful. It remained most of the time in my daughter's room and occasionally she vacated it for visitors.

One day tragedy struck when children got together to surprise me by changing that bedroom round and spring cleaning it. One hefty whack with a hammer and the cast iron support runner snapped. A more dejected and depressed bunch of children I have yet to see, than the group that met me when I came home that day. It was not a happy home coming, but all turned out well in the end and I managed to get a replacement.

Another little incident occurred some years later. The old bed springs had really seen better days, in fact, it wasn't even a spring really, it was that old mesh stuff and it sagged pitifully. For one person, it was merely a soft bed, but for two, it proved otherwise. A rather large lady with her tiny husband slept in that bed one night. In the morning, it was clear that sleep and rest had not been theirs. The lady

"HE MISTOOK MY TABLE FOR A COMMON TREE TRUNK"

wasn't too bad, just sleepy and tousled. The husband had obviously suffered. The bags under his eyes, the crick in his neck, the rats in general. "Did you not sleep too well dear?" "<u>That</u> is a very soft bed", came the reply. Say no more. The lady had rolled into the centre of the bed, and the mesh base had gasped its last. The poor husband had spent the whole night clinging to the side of the bed iron so he wouldn't roll in on top of her and suffocate either her, or himself or both of them. But all is well that ends well and we worked out a much better arrangement for them for the rest of their stay.

A short while ago, my sister-in-law got her brass bed. A magnificent specimen, given to her by one of our friends, having begun life when it was hauled from the River Thames years ago and restored. So there's romance for you. It sits adorned with ribbons, lace and pretty bags of perfumed pot pourri. Quite a retirement.

Our lace curtain era was an exciting time, worthy of a jig in the street outside our window, as we admired our handiwork. Original cream cotton lace at least thirty years old for 25p a yard and we had found it. What had we done to deserve this ecstasy, and why wasn't everyone else leaping about. Patchwork covers were a happening for us too, so were bluebells and orange blossoms. Special knitted lacy summer tops that you couldn't buy anywhere, because we made our own. Her lovely home-made bread and lovely dinners, my sewing sprees. Then what about our fireplaces. We got into rock fireplaces. They were rough sandstone rocks, slapped together and quite free because someone was disposing of a garden wall and gave us our pick. Several fireplaces were built in the end, all original and quite unique and none of them collapsed, which was a great relief because each stone weighed pounds.

Another precious and valuable item we shared was one

particular mutual friend. She came into our lives quite out of the blue with her two girls one early summer and stayed for years.

Unsinkable this one, tenacious through thick and thin, she was bulldozed into our family and once adopted, there was no escape. She endured the husband's jokes with real grit for six whole months, before she realised he was joking. After the realization dawned, six months of banter and bullying was whacked straight back in his chops and she never took him seriously again. No more scuttling into the kitchen to make his drinks when the "make me tea" siren roared forth from his corner of the lounge. No more stuttering apologies when asked "what are you lot doing here again?" Routine, that never had the same impact ever again. All those months, I used to chuckle at her futile attempts to pacify the ogre, thinking she was just playing to his silly nonsense.

Due to the coal fire and prevalence of ash, smoke, soot, etc., which automatically goes along with such a wholesome means of keeping warm, there always seemed to be an abundance of dust in our lounge. That, teamed up with armies of spiders kept me busy. I tried to be vigilant but there was always an object somewhere that escaped the damp cloth or cobweb catcher.

My dear friend and girls arrived one Friday in the middle of winter to spend the weekend with us. She was not so much "getting away from it all", more "throwing herself in at the deep end" really. On arrival I rushed her into the lounge and planted her by the fire to thaw out, and the kids all hopped about in the general mayhem of arriving. Unfortunately for my friend, one hopped onto the foot of the old standard lamp, which slowly toppled in her direction, discharging a positive cloud of dust, powder, ash, cobwebs and fossilised daddy-long-legs. I could hear her having a good cough and

splutter beyond the cloud, she became visible a little later after my frantic efforts to disperse the dust with flopping tea-cloth and huffing and puffing wildly at it. Our eyes met. "Shall I make you a nice drink, dear?" was all I could think of at the time.

This girl, my friend and companion, counterpart in our expeditions to junk shops and jumbles, January sales and nurseries. Our gardens sported ex-baths, full of weed and tadpoles, hollyhocks, lupins and as many cottage shrubs and flowers as we could afford to cram into them. She was the one who accompanied me on the really serious fruit-picking ventures, free food was an obsessions with both of us, and we both revelled in the primeval urge to "grab it while it's there."

One afternoon, we set out to one of our favourite hunting grounds, an antique (Junk) and bric-a-brac haven, out in one of the country villages. The quarry? An Indian carpet. The likelihood of there being one at our destination was a million to one, but the first thing that met our eyes was "the carpet", the one we had set our hearts on. What was to transpire here? What was to gain the ascendency? Was it to be love of friend or love of carpet? We looked at it, commented mutually on the irony of there being one there, casually strolled around the rest of the establishment, poking into corners looking for treasures. The next thing I knew, the much desired object was being "popped" into the boot of "HER" car. This is interesting, I thought, I've been carpet gazumped. Nothing more was said. I thought "Oh well" and a few other things. We drove home and shortly after, carpet, friend and friend's children drove off to their home. I contemplated for a little while, then thought "Oh well, a carpet is merely a carpet". I thought of all the nappies she'd changed for my babe (the sign of a true friend), of the fiasco's and calamities she had silently and smilingly endured and remained steadfast and loyal, of the day she had trailed across marshland and cow pats in the teaming rain, looking for frog spawn too early in the year, to placate the husband, and keep me sane, without a word of complaint. Of a whole week of my abject depression, when I was carted off to her home without a moment's notice, when the straw had broken the camel's back. Would an Indian carpet have the power to erase all this? Of course not. And why should it, when not more than a week later, there it was, lying in <u>my</u> lounge, a gift from a very dear friend.

When I think of her, I often think of a line of a poem I read many years ago. I think it's quite famous and the line was a description of a girl, maybe someone's wife. It read simply, "Trusty, dusky, vivid, true." This was her.

There was only one occasion I can remember her refusing to go along with our tide of ideas. The husband returned one morning having just dropped the children off at school, with a surprise in the boot of the car. I was rushed outside to find an adult badger, quite dead, in there. I was shocked but he insisted it was an amazing specimen, that the children would just love it. It was an opportunity for them to see a real badger and we must rush off at once and find a taxidermist. It was obviously going to be one of those days. The taxidermist we found lived in a tiny village close to my friend's home, which was just as well. It proved to be an exceptionally hot day for September, the taxidermist was out until evening and badgers in that condition do not keep too well in that heat.

The husband had a brainwave, and we invaded our friend. She came to look at our "surprise" in the boot and after a silent effort to restrain her shock - then her laughter - she asked what we were going to do with it. "Can we put it in your freezer?" asked the husband. "Would you like tea or coffee?" she asked disappearing indoors. We closed the boot and the subject of freezing the badger.

Later that evening, we all piled into our car and amidst clouds of wafting gas from the badger in the boot, we hastily made our way to the taxidermist, blaming the husband for our rather unpleasant, albeit temporary predicament.

Some weeks later, the badger, suitably stuffed and artistically encased in a glass and wooden arrangement, plus bits of bracken effect was ready for collection. Off we went with infant aged about two, to bring our acquisition home. It was put carefully onto the back seat with infant next to it and sitting at the rear end of brock. Some miles went by in silence, then infant asked: "Is it going to move?" We explained the situation as carefully and simply as possible. It was difficult for him to grasp that it wasn't alive even though it looked very much as if it was, but we did a good job, and he seemed convinced. A few miles further he said: "Is it going to eat its dinner?" We went through the explanation again patiently, embellishing it a little to make it more understandable and he finally settled down next to the badger again, but a little cautiously and suspiciously I thought. A few more miles in silence and infant finally tapped me on the shoulder. "Mummy, as I'm sitting at this end, will you tell me when he's going to do a poo please?" No wonder the poor kid was so on edge, and I must add that no explanation would satisfy him. That animal looked real to him and nothing would convince him that animals being animals, this one had better travelling habits than any other.

Old brock is still with us, to surprise the odd guest and shock the odd little toddler. His nose is a bit crisp and I got into no end of trouble when I once used my daughter's hair dryer on him, to spruce him up a bit, but part with him it seems we cannot and I often look at him and remember our introduction and the day he joined the family circle.

Christine Wright

Fire and water

That chimney's making a funny noise!! There's someone waving from the gate Mum!! Sparks shot from the chimney stack and smoke poured from the brickwork, a crowd gathered, but no one said a word, no one knocked on the door to say, they were just crowding round for the spectacle. The chimney roared, red hot cinders and soot same cascading down to the hearth and I yelled out to someone to call the fire brigade.

This was the first time of many encounters of this kind. There was something not quite right about our chimney and our neighbours' structurally. A little ledge some way up collected debris and eventually it would set alight and the fun would begin. We treated what happened in the grate with the utmost respect, but even then we had our problems.

A memorable wedding anniversary and a romantic evening to look forward to, just one more shovel full of fuel onto the fire and we'll go. Was that the old familiar roar I heard just then? The husband didn't think so. When we walked outside and saw the old familiar sparks and smoke pouring out of the stack, the husband said, "Oh it'll be OK by the time we get back". "I don't think it will my dear, get the fire brigade, I'll go back and roll up the carpet". Two hours, several firemen, fire horses and tons of wet soot later, we left the house for our evening.

Then there was the fire husband lit, that took him over two hours. The wind in the chimney that had him rushing to phone for the fire brigade. Rushing back home to discover all is well. Back to the phone to cancel the fire brigade but it was too late, they were rounding the bend in the road. In they came, out went the fire, two hours later effort hosed right out of the grate and we couldn't light it again for ages

until the sweep had been.

The pinnacle of our career in setting alight to chimneys came when we were asked to take care of lighting our neighbour's fire. Our houses were a tiny row near a farm. The wind and weather whipped across the downs, across a few fields and battered the front of the house, then came with equal force and vigour at the back, straight from the sea. We were never short of fresh air, quite the reverse, the draught could often cut you off at the ankles and certainly set your teeth chattering especially first thing in the morning. That dash from bedroom to cosy kitchen tested the strongest. So the fire in the grate was the essence of our existence. Our hearts either glow or sank with it, and our neighbours were in the same boat. They had taken a winter holiday, a fire to come home to wasn't just a cheerful welcome, it was an essential. We were happy to undertake to do it, they would do the same for us.

We had visitors at the time, all the children were playing out in the field opposite the house, we could see them and hear their laughter. It was nice for the city children to run free in the lean crisp air and they were enjoying every minute of it.

The husband insisted on dealing with the fire next door. I offered to go, because of the rather temperamental nature of the chimney situation, but he and his friend were adamant. "There's nothing to lighting a fire". A few moments went by, all seemed well. I then looked up from my book, a great pall of white and grey smoke had covered the whole street. Garden, road, field, cows and children had all completely disappeared. I could hear cars stopping on the far road and spluttering children in the field. The children gradually came into view groping their way along a fence, making their astonished way home, and a very sheepish husband came to announce that the fire brigade were on their way. He didn't stay to discuss the matter. I'd seen it all before and prepared to clear up the aftermath and explain to our neighbours. The children eventually stopped coughing and spluttering and rubbing their streaming eyes, no city fog had ever done that much damage.

Looking back, I suppose it wasn't always warm, comfortable, and easy, but it was cosy and homely and real somehow. Those great heaps of logs almost up to the ceiling, the smell of the wood and the smell of the smoke, the ash and the hissing wet coal. Clamouring to be nearest to the flickering warmth and the socks and little pants stuck in the ground to dry. Towels airing ready for the next shining naked body to appear from the bathroom to be wrapped in its glowing depths, nursery rhymes and toast, exploding chestnuts and luxurious cats. If you were ill, you got to sleep by it, bread rose by it, stories and secrets were told by it, and good friends sat quietly, or laughed, or drank wine and became nostalgic and sleepy by it. It was the glowing heart, the magnet to which we were all drawn irresistibly.

Flooding had never actually happened, storms had come and gone over the years, but we had always remained dry. Sometimes the more vigorous storms managed to lap up to our step and the children were only too delighted to wade out to the gate, but never had the water invaded our hallway, but then they had only begun building in our area in recent months.

We were out in the car and the rain was torrential and had been off and on all winter really. We drove home through a positive deluge and as the husband was in the habit often of being solidly realistic, he insisted that we must be being flooded out at home by now. That thought was met by accusations of pessimistic grouch, stop panic mongering, I don't want to hear any more of that sort of thing thank you very much. "What on earth are those people with buckets doing running up and down our garden path?" Being flooded out, we most certainly were and we had been for quite some time. My poor neighbours had been scuttling around like a family of water rats, trying to stem the flowing lake of bubbling liquid clay.

We dared not open the front door for fear of the furniture being washed right out into the back garden, so we waded around the back, donned wellies and mackintoshes and whilst the rest of the family took up their position in the bucket line, I defended the home from behind the front door with candlewick bedspreads, to block the rising tide, and mop up the worst of what had broken through. We were always ready after that with sandbags and eventually made a few adjustments in the garden to drain off any excess. The husband was always right, but on this occasion, I suspect he rather wished he hadn't been.

Water in its various forms has splashed, flowed and swept through our lives, sometimes frozen solid inside our windows or peering into the lounge in the form of a particularly handsome snowman. One particular snowman was given special privileges. The snow was thick, crisp and beckoning but chicken-pox was putting a damper on everything, there was only one answer, if we couldn't go to it, it would just have to come to us. A large plastic tablecloth and several buckets and bowls full of snow and winter's own gift of fun dwelt for a while in front of the lounge fire. The snowman had temporary accommodation in the baby's bath.

Water fights dominated much of our summer entertainment and I've seen many a sophisticated lady guest doused unmercifully by her husband and from what I could see, those husbands all had one thing in common, a great sense of achievement like they'd just done something they had been longing to do for quite some time.

Throw Me An Apple

The husband had a particular affinity for H_2O, but usually it was more the stagnant and weed-choked pond variety that he went for. I've noticed the same trait in one or two of the children.

We took a holiday one year and arrived at our destination to find a lovely bungalow set in an equally lovely garden plus pond with resident goldfish. This was a mixed blessing to some degree. We began by clearing the bungalow of all the breakables, popping them all into a safe spot rather than worry about them all week. Then came the general rules, do this and do not do that. The only fly in the ointment was the fish-pond, that couldn't be removed obviously, so the whole week was spent avoiding it, and the husband was particularly vigilant in ensuring it remained exactly as it was when we arrived and that on every occasion it was treated with the utmost respect and reverence. I think we all got fairly paranoid by the Friday before we came home. We arrived back at the bungalow on the Friday evening. It had been a glorious week, weather wonderful, accommodation still intact, tons of rock and ice-cream had been consumed and all was well.

We had decided to make the most of our last day by packing and settling everything that evening, so we could make an early start in the morning. I was undecided what to do about the dead goldfish!! The weather was hot, the water was quite low, or at least it seemed quite low. I decided to tell the guardian of the pond, the husband. "I'll go and get it", he said. I wasn't so sure that it was a good move, things had gone so well all week, but one must not interfere in these decisions, a man must do what a man must do, and I had to get on with the children's baths.

I was very tied up with my part in the proceedings, elbow deep in bubbles and shampoo and chose to ignore my name being called quietly by the husband. The call escalated in

Christine Wright

volume and urgency and I gave in and went to investigate.

Standing by the back door was an apparition, a study in mud, filth and weed, crowned with the most embarrassed angry and spluttering face imaginable. All that in his last clean tee shirt and only pair of jeans. This was a crisis and all I could do was collapse in a heap of laughter which proved contagious and we all went slowly hysterical. The silver lining was the launderette across the road and an endless supply of hot soapy water. It seems there was a loose paving slab, only one, but the husband chose that one to launch his rescue operation from. He did not actually remember falling in, only the moment he surfaced with umpteen goldfish leaping around his head. These things do happen quickly.

The sea of course has supplied and endless source of saturating and my whole family have spent endless hours in it, by it, being chased by it and swallowing it. One February they all got together to climb rocks. One fell in, splashed the next, in went that one and so on with the husband cheering them on, doing his worst and generally being an example of total irresponsibility. Someone asked who the lunatics were. I told them, "Oh, they're my family, and the biggest, loudest, and wettest is my husband." They smiled sympathetically and moved on.

One glorious day at the beach was endured through gritted teeth, due to the obnoxious behaviour of someone's dear little boy. This child spent a goodly part of the day throwing pebbles, sand and sea-weed at the rest of the children, leaping on carefully constructed sandcastles, biting, whining, complaining, howling and generally behaving in a manner that tempted the most affectionate of people to harbour an earnest desire to bury him in the sand upside-down or stick him in a rowing boat and set him adrift without paddles on the ebb tide. Everyone suffered in silence and

Christine Wright

the day wore on.

Around tea time, this little chap struck his last blow. I could not endure it a moment longer. He was very busy rubbing sand into the heads of the rest of the children. They were obviously sick and tired of it all.

An elderly Granddad was making his way up the beach, grandchild in one hand and a fair-sized bucket full of sea water, in the other. The moment of reckoning had arrived. I walked up to Granddad, smiled and asked politely if I could possibly have the contents of the bucket. With a puzzled look, he handed it over. I smiled again and thanked him profusely. The Granddad watched as I calmly waked over, tapped the offending little specimen on his head, then gave him his come-uppance in one good dousing, full in the face. "Enough is enough my dear". Then I handed the empty bucket back to an astonished Granddad and made my way back to my spot on the beach, leaving a spluttering coughing but somewhat reformed character behind me. No one said a word, the deed was done and my only regret was that I hadn't done it four hours earlier.

Wet days would attempt to drown us out but we had our ways of beating these. Our remedy was going out regardless and getting drenched. We were often joined on these ventures by the odd determined friend. It was a novelty for them to have their sandwiches dipped in rain water and their soup watered down a little, but it was a familiar experience for us, and to a large degree some of the children seem inclined to carry on the tradition.

One young lady of ours, just arriving at the "impress your beau" age, went out for a picnic day out on the downs with the revered and dashingly handsome young man plus others, including a member of the family with whom arguments were prone to arise easily. The last half cupful of congealing soup, the onset of the argument, the throwing of the last half cupful of soup into the teeth of a howling gale, which picked it up and carried it away from the annoying sister, straight into the ear and beautiful blonde hair of the desired beau. "Splat". What a shock. Indeed, what a sight. Cream of mushroom over the side of the head is not too conducive to romance. It never quite got off the ground. What the soup left, the rain soon washed away.

Surprises, gifts and games

"When I saw this, it reminded me so much of you I just had to get it", was the statement that heralded the presenting of the large old potty with its decorative bow on the handle. I peered into a mirror and wondered what had prompted that sentiment, but I did love the present, it really was just my thing, and the presenter of it did know me very well.

Gifts of clothing from the husband have been numerous, unexpected often, surprising sometimes and occasionally astonishing and perhaps a little inappropriate. I won't mention most, but there was one jumper that quite took me by surprise. In a flush of recent fatherhood, a gift it would seem was called for and it really was lovely. At another time and had I been a different shape, I would have worn it with pride. Had it been a different colour perhaps, I may well have got away with it. Sadly, due to an abundance of milk and due also to the jumper being of an exceedingly fluffy nature and coloured an almost fluorescent red, I could have been clearly seen for a radius of fifty miles, in a fog, without binoculars. I had not felt so thoroughly conspicuous ever in my life, at a time when I was desperately trying to keep a low profile, and slip by unnoticed by all. It was exchanged under a tirade of complaints from the husband, for a dark green flowery shirt, of the kind that would go undetected in a crowd, even if worn by a whale, which it was.

Often, when times were a little lean and recycling was the order of the day, clothes were often cut down and re-hashed and even chintz curtains reappeared as flowing new dresses for the girls, and also myself. The girls were quite pleased with their curtain dresses and they wore well, at least they were unique. A jumper was redesigned and served a dual role. The first creation was a tank top for the husband - the leftover sleeves became a long and well-

loved snake for my eldest son, then five years old. I was proud of my ingenuity and everyone was contented until a complication arose. Whilst waiting at the bus-stop to be taken somewhere rather special, the husband looked at the son and said to me: "I really wish he hadn't brought that with him today". "It's only his snake. I don't see why you should be so embarrassed and edgy, he loves it". "Yes, I love it too. I'm wearing the other half". The snake was hastily bundled into a carrier bag and kept out of sight for the duration of our visit.

Furniture was in the habit of being bodged up and patched too, especially the odd items I was sentimentally attached to. One such item was an old Rexine suite given to me by a very dear friend. Sadly, the sides and one back were past it, but I decided not beyond redemption. I was doing an upholstery job on it with the help of my eldest son, aged about six. We had debated at length on whether the tacks we were using would do the job, but as that was all there was at hand, we decided to get on with it.

Being the eldest son, although rather tiny, he liked to assume the role of handyman and general helper, he was also at the age where one becomes curious as to where the babies come from, and I had asked him on several occasions to ask me when we were alone, and had time to discuss these important issues in peace and privacy.

It seemed that the moment had arrived and I lived up to my promises in good faith. He passed me the tacks and listened silently and intently, hanging on every word; the upholstering progressed and I managed to make a very good job of modifying the facts of life suitably for my young listener. The deed done, I asked him what he thought, and whether I had made it clear enough. Looking at me very seriously he asked: "Why can't you put a screw in it then?" I blinked, turned purple and gasped a couple of times, whilst trying desperately to rake through my poor brain for an explanation. "What does he mean 'screw'?", I thought distractedly. Eventually, I drew a deep breath and said "What exactly do you mean, my love?" I awaited the reply with baited breath and suffering palpitations. It came. "Well, I don't think these tacks are going to hold this together for long". The relief was quite beyond explanation. I simply agreed with him.

Some things have arrived, not so much a gift, more a surprise. One was a kind of self-inflicted shock. By the time I was pregnant with number seven, having already given birth six times, I decided I knew it all and felt natural childbirth was definitely the only way and that it should all be left to the last minute. I knew what I was doing. Labour began in earnest, the husband dashed to the car, suitcase in hand. I refused to go. Back came the husband, imploring me to go at once. "I'm just gathering my thoughts dear, won't be a minute". I amble off to the car, determined to take it easy. I amble back to the house for my make-up. The husband shouts hysterically from the car. I amble back and find my make-up there. All this at 2.30 am. In January and it's freezing. "Don't panic dear", I say calmly and with the authority of a woman who knows.

We drive to the hospital and park miles from the entrance. I began to have a little less confidence in my theory due to the nature of the sudden onslaught of prolonged agony I found myself in. It was dark, it was freezing, I was yards and yards from the hospital entrance and I was about to give birth. My theory had actually worked, but I'd put it into practice in the wrong place. The car park was no place to deliver a baby and I staggered as best I could towards the maternity wing. As I walked through the door, the wheelchair was waiting. Eventually, I was hauled out of it again and my clothes were being unzipped and disposed of as I was escorted rapidly into the labour room. "How long have I got?" I asked. "When you're ready to push, we're ready to catch dear", came the reply, and they meant it.

Whilst insisting over the years that the children are always sporting losers and no sulking, arguing or free-for-alls occur due to having lost at games, the husband has always been the first to set an example, mainly of being positively determined to win at all costs thus eliminating the necessity to sulk, argue or scrap.

At children's parties, he really comes into his own, shoving kids in all directions at musical chairs and then having the gall to wait for the prize at the end. "Who's that chap laying on the floor outside the pass-the-parcel ring?" I heard at one event. I looked across the room and there he was, flat on the floor behind our kids, with his arms stretched out into the ring trying to catch the parcel as it went by.

Field games in general have to be played by "his" rules and the first half hour is spent being put in your place, deafened by the rules bellowed out twenty times, (so you don't forget) then he proceeds to cheat his way to winning.

Football is a fiasco whilst he blunders, bellows and fouls his way from goal to goal. Then if all else fails, he feigns injury and rolls around clutching a shin and yelling, face distorted with pseudo agony. This was his tactic during one game and no one took a scrap of notice to his nonsense. Finally, I went over and insisted he stop his disgusting performance and get on with the game, the performance persisted however and finally after a trip to the casualty department at the local hospital, he reappeared from the plaster room, encased up to his thigh and looking very sorry for himself. Met with gales of laughter from all and absolutely no sympathy, he was

Christine Wright

confined to a wheel-chair for weeks and I was condemned to pushing it, a fitting penalty for my gross lack of respect. Actually, I had a lot of trouble with that wheelchair. Every time the front wheels hit even the slightest irregularity in the pavement, the husband was thrust forward at high speed and was reduced to a nervous wreck in no time. After all my years of pram pushing, I never got the mastery over that dreadful contraption. We ended up dumping the shopping or luggage into it whilst the husband hobbled along behind, a kind of Zimmer on wheels.

Board games have been numerous and my vacuum cleaners have chocked on varieties of coloured counters, dice, plastic shapes and cardboard bits and pieces until I've reached the limit of my endurance and descended upon them, refuse sack in hand and disposed of every item of board game I could find in the vicinity of my home and domain. They gradually reappeared again of course and the process was repeated many times.

I never exactly shone at board games, but of course the husband never failed to master them and proceeded to make it too excruciating to play against him, as your counters were pinged into infinity, your chess men were laid low, your dice never did what his dice did and your self-esteem disintegrated under his tirade of bragging, whilst you crawled or stomped off into the kitchen to pay your penalty for being useless, by making him another cup of tea.

There was one occasion only that the boot was on the other foot. It was a ridiculous game with red and blue counters, and I just couldn't grasp it. I tried and tried. I was blundering my way through yet another session of it and suddenly the husband gasped "you've won!!!" "Have I?" I asked. "How did that happen, what did I do?" But he couldn't reply, in fact he couldn't speak at all. Due to the shock of being beaten by the biggest dumb in the household, he was in the grip of an asthma attack. I'd never seen anything like it before. To my knowledge, he had never suffered with asthma. He continued to gasp and turn purple and I suggested he go to bed and lie down to get over it. Of he went. I made him a hot drink.

I took his drink up to him feeling sure he must be over the shock and on the road to recovery by now. What a sight met my eyes as I entered the bedroom. The husband in bed, clutching the bedclothes, still purple and gasping and now covered from head to foot on a bright red rash. I gave him his drink, told him I thought this performance was absolutely outrageous and made a private vow never to win again.

Another occasion where the husband came home a conquering hero occurred after a table tennis match at his place of work.

The husband and his friends went for the "ping-pong" in deadly earnest and pounds in weight were lost, cartilages were damaged and reputations were won and lost; bats of intricate abilities were purchased at no little cost and wives were told of great battles won against unbelievable odds.

The husband arrived home from work one evening looking a little ragged at the edges and at closer inspection I discovered an injury across his eyebrow sporting several stitches, and the evidence of splattered blood. I was shocked. What had happened to my love? What dreadful skirmish had taken place to produce such an injury? What bully had taken advantage of his mild good mannered disposition..? "I hit myself on the head with my table tennis bat, my love!!!" "Get indoors, your dinner's on the table". Sympathy and hero worship dissolved without trace.

Tess surprised us a few times. A roly-poly white bull-dog full

Throw Me An Apple

Christine Wright

"HE SLID OFF THE TABLE STRAIGHT INTO HER GAPING JAWS"

of love for the family and bounce, and character, of which I'm sure we'll never experience again, plodded around after us constantly, adoring our very presence, and it wasn't until we had to take her for a visit to the vets' one time that we discovered she had quite a healthy appetite for other doggies and certainly suffered canine fools badly. Fortunately, the husband was awake at the time of our enlightening and had her on a short lead. We, however, continued to love her dearly and our hearts melted at just one glance from those great brown eyes.

Infant was particularly attached to her and they were close companions. The closer the better was infant's opinion. One day having been washed and dressed for a special event, he was allowed out of sight for two seconds and disappeared completely. He turned up some time later, having been discovered laying side by side with Tess, arm around her in her kennel. Two contented faces beaming out of the kennel door, pressed together and both with that distinctive canine aroma, another bath was called for.

Tess, when small, was taken for a stroll that turned out to be a hike by number four, then in her early teens. The walk was going well. Number four's friend accompanied her with her dog Tilly, and Tilly and Tess got on fine. It was a lovely, bright, warm summer evening and all was quite idealistic until Tess suddenly collapsed, legs in air. Tess was not designed to go on hikes, only on strolls. Tess was exhausted, number four was horrified. Patrons from a nearby public house rushed in and out with ash trays full of cold water to revive the prostrate Tess. She drank dozens of them whilst number four hopped around in a state of panic and anxiety, being only too well aware of the consequences of returning home with an ex-bulldog. All ended well, however, and I didn't actually become acquainted with this tale until a couple of years after the event, a suitable length of time to allow the dust to settle, it probably took number four that long to get over the shock.

Tess loved the new kitten, but we didn't give her credit for her depth of affection then the tiny black kitten slid off the table, straight into her gaping jaws, several people screamed, others leapt to the kitten's rescue, still others froze rigid as their imaginations ran riot and the kitten's owner burst into tears. Tess merely proceeded to place the adored one onto the floor and slobber all over it, prod it around with her snuffly black nose a little, sneeze once or twice, then lose interest all together. We all heaved a tremendous sigh of relief and the sobbing owner proceeded to recover and attempt to dry off her saturated darling. We never concerned ourselves with the kitten's safety again and the little kitten never failed to take every advantage of Tessa's good nature.

A drinking straw in a large pink milkshake gave me a little surprise on one occasion, not to say a little pain and some embarrassment. After a rather harassing shopping spree, a treat was called for, and there it was, a delicious pink thick, creamy milkshake. In a tired haze, and gazing adoringly at the husband who had accompanied me on this rather wearing trip to the shops, I lifted the milkshake to my lips. Sadly it missed my lips and the straw proceeded on up my left nostril. My eyes watered somewhat and I was shocked but quickly thought, it won't be too bad, if no one has noticed and as I hadn't actually screamed, it could have been discreetly overlooked. No chance. A mesmerised and highly amused expression on the face of a young gentleman sitting not far off confirmed my worst fears. I can never make a complete idiot of myself without someone there to witness the event. I might just as well give in to my destiny.

So there we are, at least I've made a start and as time goes on and the memories make their presence felt, I've no doubt there will be more, so "throw me an apple" and give me a minute to think.

Throw Me An Apple